Julia Wall
Heath McKenzie

NELSON
A Cengage Company

Australia • Brazil • Mexico • Singapore • United Kingdom • United States

Nico's List

Fast Forward
Gold Level 22

Text: Julia Wall
Illustrations: Heath McKenzie
Editor: Cameron Macintosh
Design: Karen Mayo
Series design: James Lowe
Production controller: Seona Galbally
Audio recordings: Juliet Hill, Picture Start
Spoken by: Matthew King and Abbe Holmes
Reprint: Jennifer Foo

Text © 2007 Cengage Learning Australia Pty Limited
Illustrations © 2007 Cengage Learning Australia Pty Limited

Copyright Notice
This Work is copyright. No part of this Work may be reproduced, stored in a retrieval system, or transmitted in any form or by any means without prior written permission of the Publisher. Except as permitted under the *Copyright* 1968, for example any fair dealing for the purposes of private study, research criticism or review, subject to certain limitations. These limitations include: Restricting the copying to a maximum of one chapter or 10% of this book, whichever is greater; Providing an appropriate notice and warning with the copies of the Work disseminated; Taking all reasonable steps to limit access these copies to people authorised to receive these copies; Ensuring you hold appropriate Licences issued by the Copyright Agency Limited ("CAL"), supply remuneration notice to CAL and pay any required fees.

ISBN 978 0 17 012684 7
ISBN 978 0 17 012681 6 (set)

Cengage Learning Australia
Level 7, 80 Dorcas Street
South Melbourne, Victoria Australia 3205
Phone: 1300 790 853

Cengage Learning New Zealand
Unit 4B Rosedale Office Park
331 Rosedale Road, Albany, North Shore NZ 0632
Phone: 0800 449 725

For learning solutions, visit **cengage.com.au**

Printed in Australia by Ligare Pty Ltd
6 7 8 9 10 11 12 21 20 19 18 17

Evaluated in independent research by staff from the Department of Language, Literacy and Arts Education at the University of Melbourne.

Nico's List

Julia Wall
Heath McKenzie

Contents

Chapter 1 **The Tickets** 4
Chapter 2 **The List** 12
Chapter 3 **Cancelled!** 18
Chapter 4 **The CD** 22

Chapter 1

The Tickets

"Why are you cutting your toenails in here!" Maria yelled at me in the living room. "That is so gross!"

Then she slammed the door and stomped off to her room.

I knew why my sister was in
such a bad mood.
Her favourite band, the Sci-fi Zombies,
were coming to town
and she didn't have tickets.

I turned on the radio.
They were playing
a Sci-fi Zombies song.
It was one of Maria's favourites.
Luckily for me, it was the end
of the song.
"Great news, everyone,"
the announcer was saying.
"Be the ninth caller through
and win a double pass to see
the Sci-fi Zombies live in concert
this Friday!"

The Tickets

Suddenly, I had an idea.
I picked up the phone
and entered the station number
into speed dial.

A few minutes later,
I knocked on Maria's door.
She was lying on her bed,
mooning over a poster of Johnny Alien,
the lead singer of the Sci-fi Zombies.

"Hey, Maria," I said. "Guess what?"

The Tickets

"Go away," she scowled,
and turned on her side.

"I just called Radio Rad," I said,
"and won a double pass
to the Sci-fi Zombies concert."

Nico's List

Maria turned around.
"You did not," she said.

"I did too. They're sending me the tickets today," I replied.

"But you don't even like them!" she said.

"No," I said, "but you do, so if you're my slave until Friday, I'll give you the tickets."

"What do I have to do?" asked Maria.

The Tickets

I knew she'd give anything
to see Johnny Alien live.
"There are my jobs for a start," I said.
"This week I'm on kitchen stuff."

"I can do that," said Maria quickly.
"What else?"

Cool, I thought.
This was going to be a piece of cake.
"I don't know yet," I said.
"I'll let you know."

Chapter 2

The List

That night, Maria did my chores
while I put my feet up
and watched TV.
It was great.

The next morning, I asked Maria
for a ride to school.
We go to different schools,
and normally I take the bus.

"I'll be late!" she said.

The Sci-fi Zombies tickets
had already arrived by courier.
I pulled them out of my pocket.
"Not if we leave now," I said.
"And remember, you have to be
my slave if you want to see
your beloved!"
I waved the tickets in front of her.

"Johnny Alien is not my beloved!"
But Maria turned red and picked up
her car keys.

Nico's List

It was great going to school
in Maria's car, instead of by bus.
By the time I got to school,
I'd thought of more things
that Maria could do before Friday.

The List

I made a list.

1. Clean my soccer boots.
2. Wash my soccer gear.
3. Drop me off at the gym.
4. Help me with my homework.
5. Do anything else that I think of between now and Friday.

That night, I showed Maria the list.

"This had better be a good concert,"
she said.
Then she went and got
my soccer boots from the hallway.
"Oh, gross, Nico!" she said,
looking at all the dried-on mud.
"When was the last time
you cleaned them?"

The List

For the next two days,
my life was awesome.
Maria did everything on the list,
which meant I got time
to put my feet up.

Chapter 3

Cancelled!

On Thursday night,
Maria knocked on my door.
"What is it, slave?" I asked jokingly.

"I'm no longer your slave," said Maria.
"The concert's been cancelled.
I just heard it on the radio."
Then she ran back to her room.

Cancelled!

Oh well, I thought,
it was good while it lasted.
I decided to go and thank Maria
for all the stuff she'd done.

She was face down on her bed,
and I could tell she was crying.
"What is it?" she asked.

"I came to say thanks," I said,
"for helping me with my homework
and all the other stuff.
I'm sorry about the concert."

"Yeah, right."
Maria turned away from me.

Cancelled!

I went back to my room,
and the phone rang.
It was Radio Rad,
saying sorry about the tickets
and offering me
something else instead.
I knew exactly what I was going to do
with what they gave me.

Chapter 4

The CD

The next day, the courier was back.
"Hey, Maria," I said.
"I've got something for you."

"Go away," she said.
"I don't want to talk to you."

"Go on," I said. "Open it."

Maria looked at the parcel.
I could tell she was curious.

The CD

"Oh well," I said,
pretending to leave.
"If you don't want to listen to
the new Sci-fi Zombies double CD,
I'll listen to it myself."

'Mouse-traps' was the Sci-fi Zombies'
new CD.
I knew Maria was saving for it.

Maria grabbed the parcel from me and ripped it open.
"Did you get this from Radio Rad?" she asked.

I nodded.
"I guess I'm just lucky," I said.
"Having you for a sister," I added.

"Oh, don't be such an idiot!" she said.

But I could tell she was over the moon.